WORKIN' NOON TO FIVE

THE OFFICIAL WORKPLACE QUIZ BOOK

A SHOEBOX GREETINGS Book
(A tiny little division of Hallmark)

Andrews and McMeel
A Universal Press Syndicate Company
Kansas City

Other SHOEBOX GREETINGS Books from Andrews and McMeel
(A tiny little division of Hallmark)

Raiders of the Lost Bark
Workin' Noon to Five
Don't Worry, Be Crabby!

written by:

Chris Brethwaite, Bill Bridgeman, Bill Gray, Allyson Jones, Kevin Kinzer, Mark Oatman, Scott Oppenheimer, Dee Ann Stewart, Dan Taylor, Richard Warwick and Myra Zirkle.

cartoons by:

Vincent Andriani

 For information write Andrews and McMeel, a Universal Press Syndicate Company, 4900 Main Street, Kansas City, Missouri 64112.

ISBN: 0-8362-1730-6

Library of Congress Catalog Card Number: 93-71870

A SPITEFUL BOSS DOES ALL HE CAN TO MAKE YOUR LIFE MISERABLE.

YOU CAN'T HELP BUT WONDER:

A. Is he under stress at home?

B. Does he have a proper diet?

C. How long could he hold his breath underwater?

IN CASE OF SOME NATURAL EMERGENCY, YOU'VE ALREADY PLANNED:

A. A safe, rapid evacuation route from the office.
B. Where to seek temporary shelter.
C. Who you'd choose as a mate to repopulate the earth.

TRUE OR FALSE?

HARD WORK PAYS OFF.

TRUE! Once you get that petty cash box open, it's *yours*!

Some companies provide an employee cafeteria. **This is especially appreciated by:**

A. Busy, deadline-conscious employees.

B. Bargain-minded meal shoppers.

C. People who actually liked bone-dry fish sticks and rubbery lime gelatin in junior high school.

In your opinion, filing is:

A. An unpleasant but necessary task.

B. A function you will gladly perform if it is helpful to others.

C. A must if you want your nails to maintain an attractive appearance.

PARKING LOT MAZE
FIND YOUR WAY TO YOUR PARKING SPOT.
WHERE THE CHAUFFEUR WASHES THE LIMO.
COVERED SPOT FOR COMPANY CAR.
VIP PARKING.
GUEST PARKING.
PARKING SPOT UNDER REPAIR.
WHERE THE JANITOR PARKS.
ALTERNATE PARKING FOR JANITOR-- JUST IN CASE.
ONLY SPOT LEFT. OFTEN REFERRED TO AS "LAND OF POTHOLES AND GLASS SHARDS."

ELEVATOR ETIQUETTE requires that, if you see a frenzied coworker rushing to catch the closing doors of your car, you should always:

A. Hold the door open.

B. Move to the back of the car to make room.

C. Fake holding the "door open" button until seconds before the doors slam shut on the sucker's nose then let him hear your laughter crackling up the empty shaft.

WHEN YOU HEAR THE WORDS **"UPPER MANAGEMENT,"** YOU IMMEDIATELY THINK OF:

A. Your long-range goal.

B. Your next promotion.

C. A boss voodoo doll riddled with pins.

WHAT DO YOU SEE IN THE ILLUSTRATION AT RIGHT?

A. A wall clock.
B. That it is nearly quitting time.
C. Nothing. You left 20 minutes ago.

A. Workin' 9 to 5.
B. Whistle While You Work.
C. Taps.

A. Half empty.

B. Half full.

C. Decaf! You need caffeine in your system NOW and some inconsiderate jerk let THAT pot burn dry!

FIND THE HIDDEN OBJECTS!

The following objects are hidden in the drawing of a company picnic on the facing page: A bowling ball, a lamp, a stoplight, and a happy employee.

CAN YOU FIND THEM ?

FOOLED YOU! YOU'D NEVER FIND A HAPPY EMPLOYEE AT A COMPANY PICNIC.

When the copy machine breaks down, you think:

A. I'm sure it will be repaired promptly.

B. I hope this doesn't cause any inconvenience.

C. Dang! Only one check this payday.

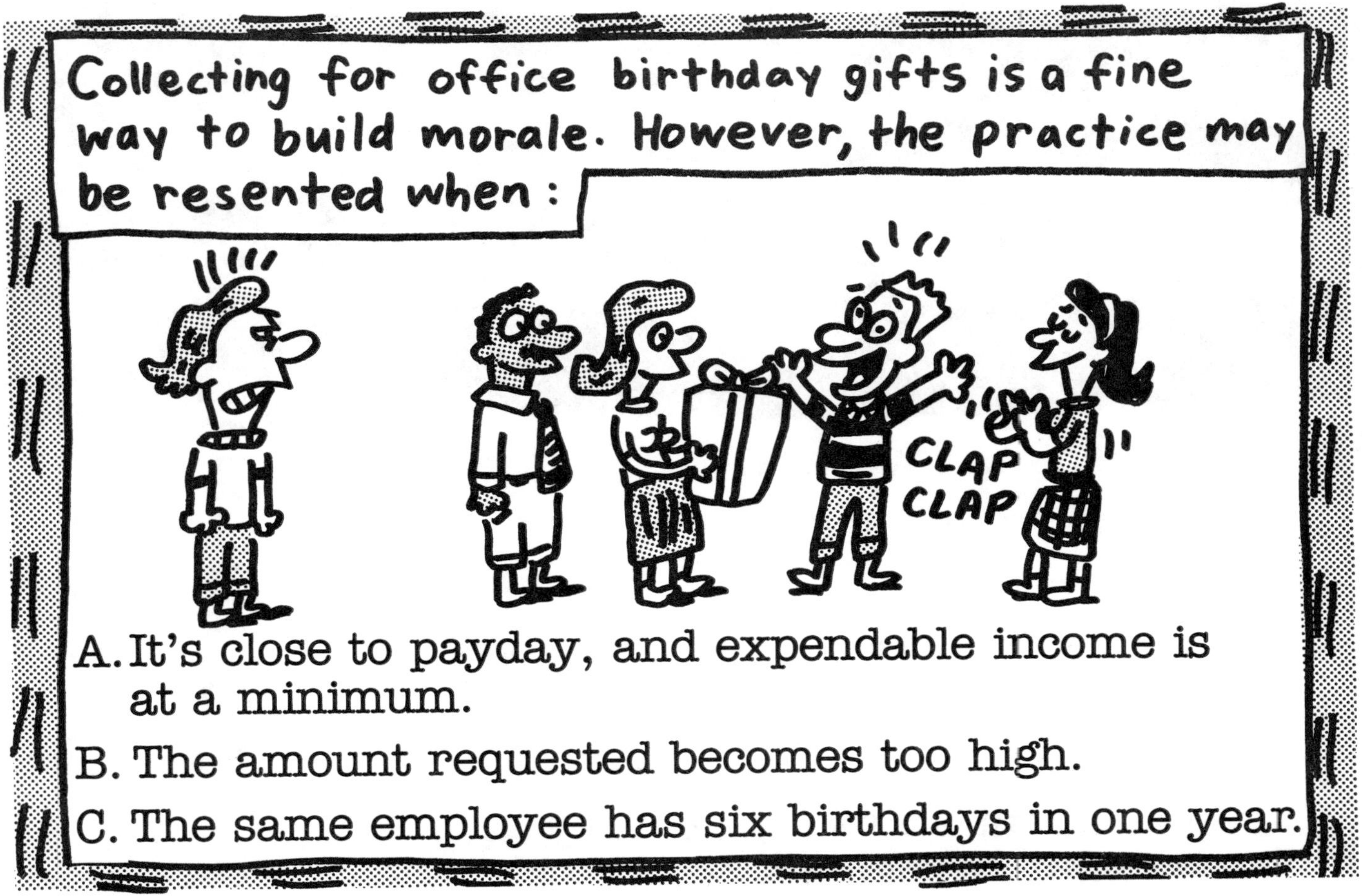
Collecting for office birthday gifts is a fine way to build morale. However, the practice may be resented when:
CLAP CLAP
A. It's close to payday, and expendable income is at a minimum.
B. The amount requested becomes too high.
C. The same employee has six birthdays in one year.

Should you ever decide to change jobs, you must keep in mind that not all benefit packages are equal. Which of the following are good benefits and which are not?

	Good	Not good
1. Paid medical coverage.	☐	☐
2. Free aspirin after major surgery.	☐	☐
3. Paid vacation.	☐	☐
4. Sunday afternoons off after 10 years.	☐	☐
5. Stock options.	☐	☐
6. Free brochure from the hotel where management stayed when they gambled away your retirement fund.	☐	☐

A. A busy hive of productive bees making delicious honey.

B. A thriving farm of ants cooperating to move obstacles many times their own combined weight.

C. A turnip squeezed in a vise until it sheds a drop of blood.

"Goodie Day" is:

A. Any day someone brings in treats.
B. A good excuse to go off your diet.
C. The boss's retirement day.

HALLOWEEN AT THE OFFICE CAN BE CHALLENGING BECAUSE:

A. It's tough to come up with a creative costume that's appropriate for work.
B. It's tough to avoid all those tempting sugary treats.
C. It's tough to tell those dressed as undead zombies from the employees who look like undead zombies every day.

CONNECT THE DOTS AND FIND OUT WHAT HAPPENED TO THE LAST PERSON WHO ASKED FOR A RAISE.

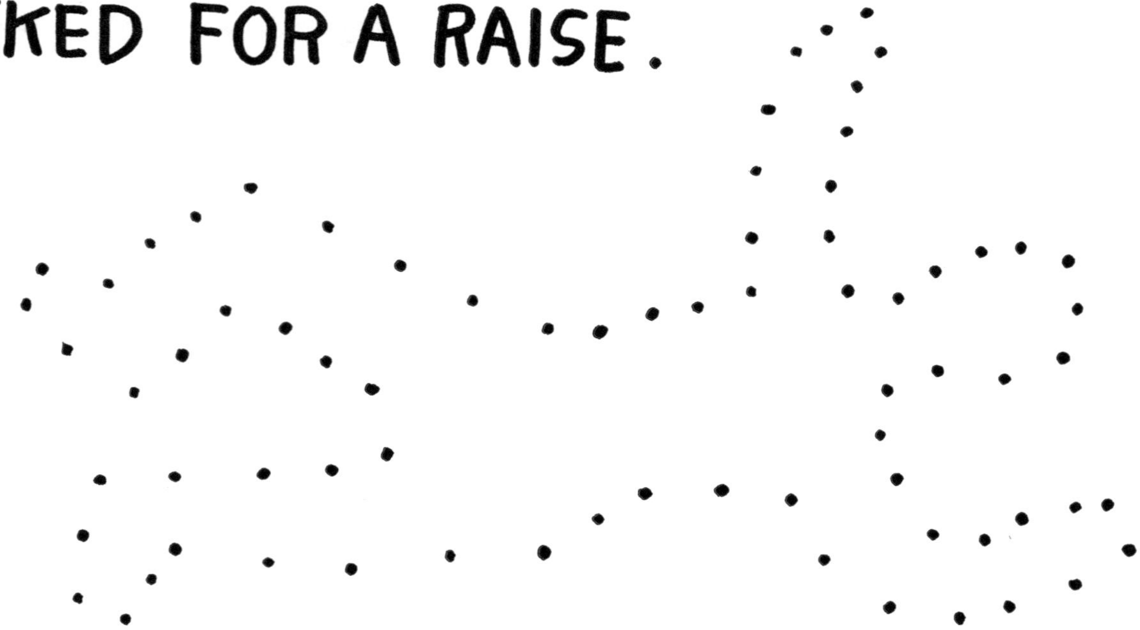

A. Valuable information is not lost.

B. Key messages can be transcribed and filed.

C. You can do your life-of-the-party "Bogart Meets Rocky" impression, then call your own number to hear it.

YOU CARRY A LARGE LEATHER-BOUND APPOINTMENT BOOK:

A. To remind you of important meetings.

B. To recall coworkers' birthdays and anniversaries.

C. Because when you carry it, people will think you're on your way to an important conference rather than sneaking out to play nine holes of golf.

BRAINTEASER! WHICH MEMBER OF UPPER MANAGEMENT IS NOT LIKE THE OTHERS?

ANSWER The third one from the left has a teeny-tiny little heart, unlike the others who have no heart at all.

WHERE YOU WORK, THE TERM "DRESSING FOR SUCCESS" MEANS:

A. An expensive dark suit.

B. Well-shined shoes.

C. A paper hat to match your one-size-fits-all smock.

WHICH OF THE FOLLOWING PRACTICES DO YOU FEEL WOULD MOST BENEFIT THE CLIMATE OF AMERICAN BUSINESS ?

A. Communism.

B. Socialism.

C. Voyeurism.

MATCH THE WORK CHALLENGE WITH THE PROPER RESPONSE.

WORK CHALLENGE	RESPONSE
A. A new project gives workers an opportunity to grow.	A. Call in sick.
B. The boss initiates an incentive program.	B. Call in sick.
C. You're training a new employee.	C. Call in sick.
D. The vending machine is out of cupcakes.	D. Call in sick.

YOU RIDE A BIKE TO WORK EACH DAY BECAUSE:

A. You're concerned about the environmental impact of rapidly increasing traffic.

B. It's fun to see the scenery whizzing by in the fresh morning air.

C. Since your last raise, you've moved up from the rickety skateboard.

A. A concise record of the past year's successes.

B. A valuable comparative analysis.

C. The most outrageous work of science fiction since "Attack of the 50-foot Accountant."

DURING THOSE FEW BRIEF MOMENTS WHEN YOU'RE NOT HARD AT WORK, YOU SOMETIMES FANTASIZE:
A. You have been named C.E.O., and your brilliant initiatives turn the business around.
B. You have been relocated to Tahiti.
C. You are strangling that person who always says "Workin' hard, or hardly workin'?"

STORY PROBLEM:

Wally's Work Day

Wally leaves home at the usual time, rushing through the door of his office just in time to clock in at 8 a.m. He spends the following 45 minutes running to the bakery for donuts and coffee, and enjoying them at his desk. He works until 9 a.m., then spends 20 minutes in the bathroom with the Wall Street Journal.

He works until 9:30, then walks to the watercooler where he meets Fred. They discuss the sporting results from the weekend. Wally is back at his desk by 10.

He soon finds that his typewriter is out of ribbon. On his way to the supply closet, he passes the desk of Betty, a new secretary. Wally arrives back at his desk about 11:15, works until 11:30, then breaks for lunch.

QUESTION: HOW MUCH TIME DID WALLY ACTUALLY SPEND WORKING?

ANSWER: TOO MUCH! HE FORGOT TO TAKE HIS COFFEE BREAK.

YOUR COWORKER HAS AN ANNOYING HABIT OF DRUMMING HIS FINGERS ON HIS DESK IN TIME TO HIS RADIO.

YOU CAN BEST DEAL WITH THIS BY:

A. Slamming his fingers in the office door.

B. Slamming his fingers in the file cabinet.

C. Slamming his fingers in his desk drawer.

ANSWER : A FAKE COUGH.

A. A more than adequate income for the rest of your life.

B. Continued medical coverage.

C. You never have to work in this cesspool of greed and indifference again.

STANDARD SUPPLIES FOR ANY PRODUCTIVE AREA INCLUDE:

A. Adequate lighting.

B. A clean, uncluttered work space.

C. A big calendar featuring lovable pictures of chimpanzees saying goofy things.

Building personal relationships between employees can help improve morale. Which are the appropriate relationship-building things to say when you see a family photo on a coworker's desk?

	APPROPRIATE	INAPPROPRIATE
A. "Goodlookin' bunch!"	☐	☐
B. "My, what a family resemblance!"	☐	☐
C. "You must be proud!"	☐	☐
D. "Whoa! No wonder you constantly volunteer for overtime."	☐	☐

YOU LIKE TO GREET NEW EMPLOYEES FIRST THING SO THAT:
A. They will feel welcome.
B. They will feel like part of the team.
C. They will be so confused by your babbled misinformation that they'll mess up their jobs and never be a threat to your gravy position.

IF THE BOSS CALLS YOU INTO HIS OFFICE, IT MEANS:

A. Your signature is required on an important document.

B. The boss would like your opinion on something, because that opinion is so highly valued.

C. The boss's trash can is full again.

TRUE or FALSE?

You have always avoided office romances because they detract from a professional working environment and go against your own high moral standards.

FALSE! You have always avoided them because nobody at work finds you even remotely attractive.

You "brown-bag" your lunch so that:

A. You can save money.

B. You can use up those leftovers from home.

C. You can inflate the bag and pop it behind sleeping coworkers.

AN IMPORTANT PART OF YOUR JOB IS KNOWING HOW TO HANDLE:
A. A power breakfast.
B. A power lunch.
C. A power mower.

WHAT DO YOU SEE IN THIS PICTURE?

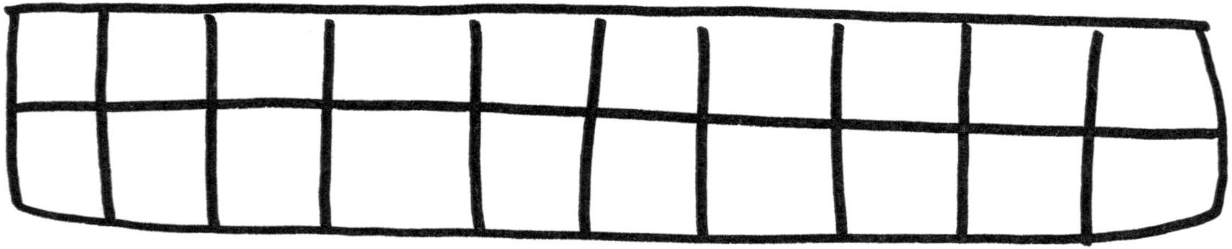

A. Boxed inventory, neatly stacked on a pallet and ready for shipping.

B. A modern, two-story office building.

C. Close-up of your clenched teeth after the boss tells you to come in on Saturday.

THE OFFICE SNITCH ACCUSES YOU OF MAKING PERSONAL LONG-DISTANCE PHONE CALLS AND USING OFFICE EQUIPMENT FOR YOUR OWN BENEFIT.

THIS SURPRISES YOU BECAUSE:

A. You have high ethical standards.
B. You consider yourself an example to others.
C. You were sure that boot-licking dork didn't see you.

READING COMPREHENSION

OUR FRIEND THE VENDING MACHINE

The vending machine is our friend. When our work load seems too heavy and we need a short break, we can go to the vending machine. There we will see a variety of snacks, including fresh fruit, crackers and sweets with colorful names like "Wing Dings," "Snackies," and "Fudge Dogs."

Yes, the vending machine is truly our friend.

WHAT IS THE MAIN THOUGHT IN THE PRECEDING PARAGRAPH?

A. The vending machine is our friend.

B. The vending machine is a good place to go for a short break from work.

C. If that stupid thing takes my quarter without giving me a candy bar again, I'm gonna put my foot through it!

YOUR LONG-TERM CAREER GOAL IS:

A. To rise to an upper management position.

B. To be recognized for your outstanding work.

C. To have the coffee mug with the funniest saying on it.

Connect The Dots!

1. 2.

WHAT DO YOU SEE?

A. A flat sales record.

B. One of the lines in a steno pad.

C. Your career path.

YOU respect the folks in accounting, but you don't interact with them because:

A. You know they're busy, busy, busy.

B. Their detailed work requires intense concentration.

C. You're afraid geekiness could be contagious.

THE QUESTION WHICH YOUR COWORKERS MOST OFTEN CHALLENGE THEMSELVES WITH IS:

A. "What if ...?"

B. "Why not?"

C. "Huh?"

WHAT'S WRONG WITH THIS PICTURE ?

ANSWER: The meeting has gone over 10 minutes, and an employee is still awake.

YOUR DEPARTMENT'S SOFTBALL TEAM PROVES:

A. "Teamwork" extends beyond the office.

B. Competition can build character.

C. People can hold a grudge for years against the goat who dropped an easy fly ball and cost them the league championship.

THE BOSS HAS JUST CHOSEN YOU TO WORK ON A SPECIAL PROJECT. THIS IS PROBABLY BECAUSE:

A. The boss has great confidence in your capabilities.

B. You're the kind of "take charge" person who can get things done.

C. For some reason, your boss does not want this project to succeed.

What do you see in this picture?

A. Cookie and popcorn left over from this week's goodie day.
B. The sun and clouds as seen from your office window.
C. Top view of your wastebasket after shooting baskets all afternoon.

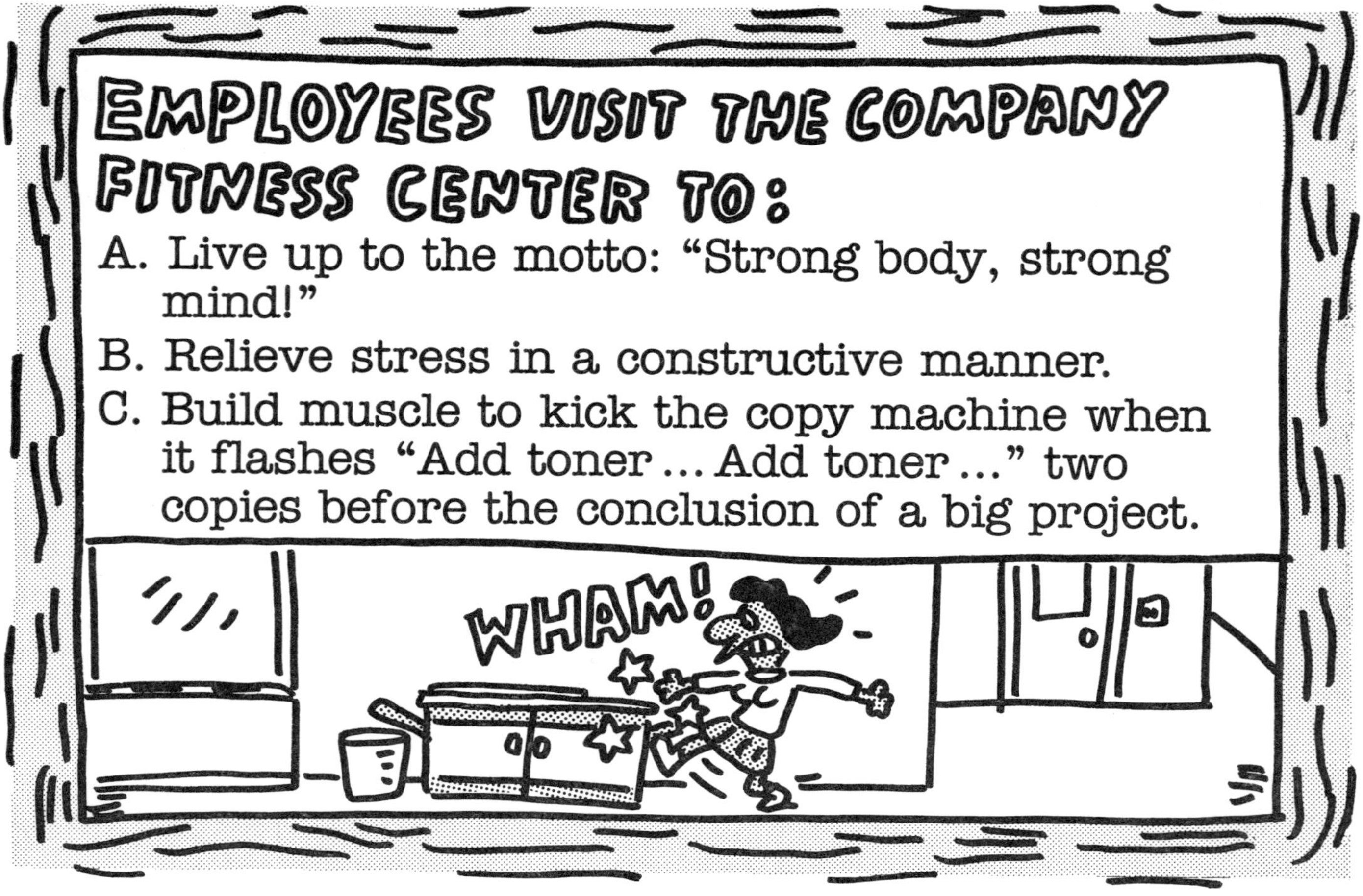
EMPLOYEES VISIT THE COMPANY FITNESS CENTER TO:
A. Live up to the motto: "Strong body, strong mind!"
B. Relieve stress in a constructive manner.
C. Build muscle to kick the copy machine when it flashes "Add toner ... Add toner ..." two copies before the conclusion of a big project.
WHAM!

WHICH DIAGRAM REPRESENTS THE CORRECT USE OF PIPED-IN MUSIC?

— FIG. A. —

— FIG. B. —

WHILE APPROACHING THE DESIGNATED SMOKING AREA AT THE OFFICE, YOU SHOULD:

A. Smile and say, "Good morning, all!"

B. Walk around the area so you don't disturb anyone.

C. Cough, choke, and wheeze loudly while pointing at your lungs and making bomb noises like you did in third grade.

*YOUR BONUS DOLLAR:

A PIE CHART.

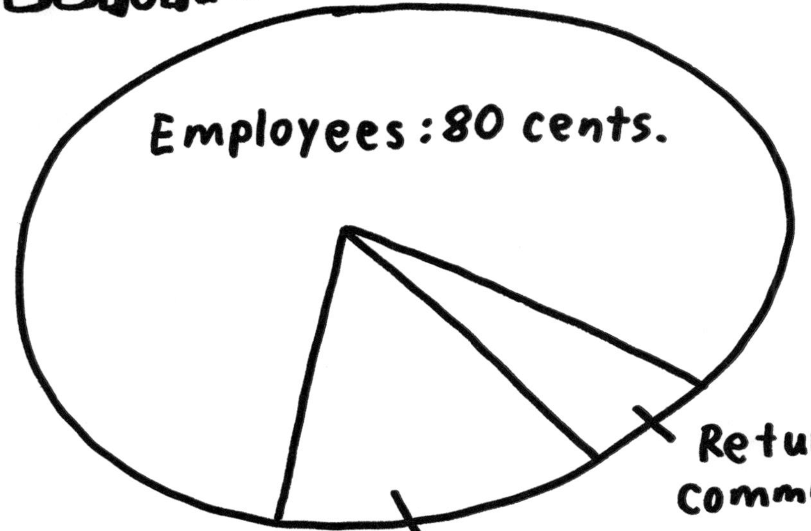

* KEEP IN MIND: IT'S ONLY ONE DOLLAR.

THE HISTORICAL FIGURE WHO WOULD BEST FIT IN AS A MANAGER OF YOUR COMPANY WOULD BE:
A. George Washington.
B. Abraham Lincoln.
C. Calamity Jane.

What do you see in this picture?

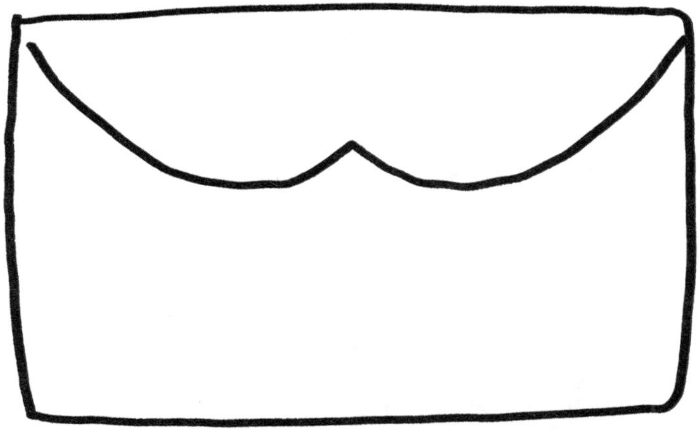

A. The back of a standard #10 business envelope.

B. A graph showing last quarter's gross profits.

C. What the office copier produced after you sat on it at last year's Christmas party.

YOU RECEIVE A GOLD WATCH FROM THE COMPANY. THIS INDICATES:

A. You are a valued employee.

B. A profitable year is rewarded.

C. Security cameras caught the coworker who stole your gold watch.

MATCHING

WHO GETS WHICH TRIP?

A. Sample cuisine in Italy.

B. Study surf on Maui.

C. Evaluate Bahama hotels.

D. Check fashions in France.

E. Measure toxin levels in various deserted dumpsites.

A. The boss.

B. You.

C. The boss's kid.

D. The boss's nephew.

E. The boss's golfing buddy.

YOU FIND A PENNY UNDER YOUR CHAIR AT WORK.

YOU IMMEDIATELY THINK:

A. This is my lucky day!

B. Those cleaning people are lax!

C. The Christmas bonuses are here!
The Christmas bonuses are here!

What's wrong with this picture?

ANSWER: The computer is actually working.

THE DOOR TO YOUR OFFICE HAS A SIGN THAT READS:

A. Corporate Executive Office.
B. Appointments Required.
C. Men.

CONNECT THE DOTS TO DETERMINE THE GOAL UPPER MANAGEMENT HOPES TO ACCOMPLISH IN THE COMING YEAR.

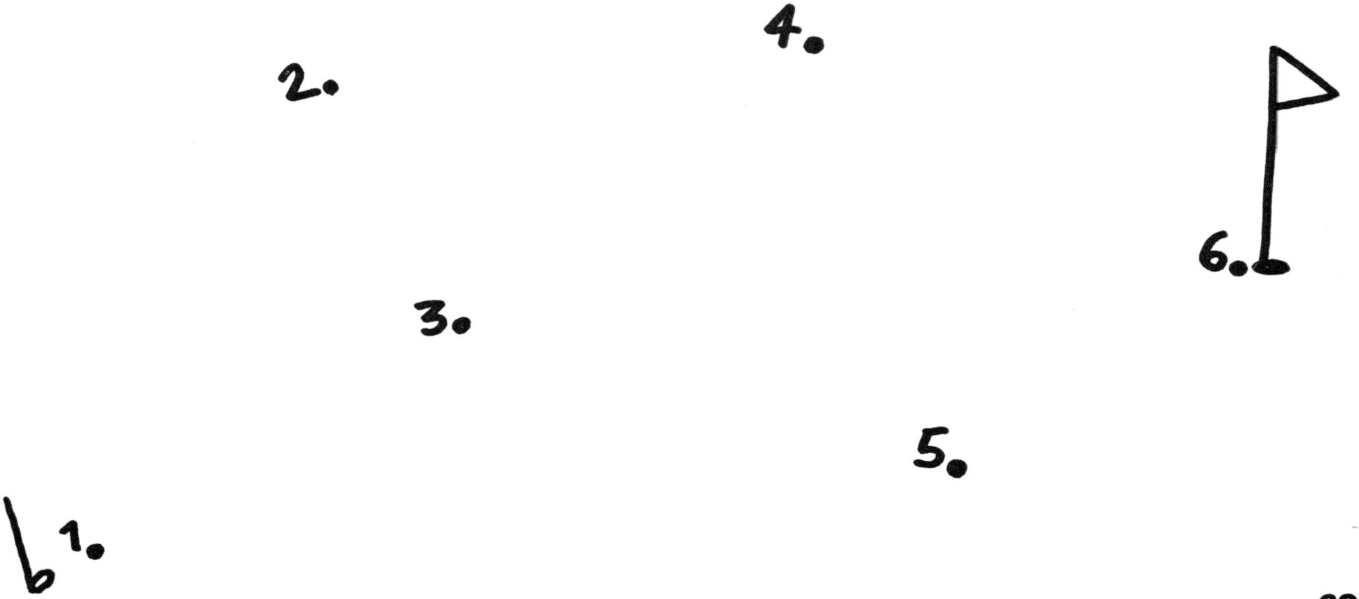

THE BOSS WALKS PAST YOUR DESK AND SAYS, "**I THINK YOU NEED A RAISE.**" THIS PROBABLY MEANS:

A. Your fine work has not gone unnoticed.

B. There will be more money in your next paycheck.

C. Maintenance will be around later to increase the height of your chair.

TRUE OR FALSE ?
MANAGEMENT ADVISES YOU TO AVOID "RED TAPE" BECAUSE THEY WANT THE PROCESSES WHERE YOU WORK TO BE EFFICIENT AND STREAMLINED.
FALSE!
THEY WANT TO AVOID "RED TAPE" BECAUSE IT COSTS A HALF-CENT MORE THAN TRANSPARENT TAPE.

IF YOU HAD TO PICK A FUN, LIGHT-HEARTED NICKNAME FOR YOUR BOSS, IT WOULD MOST LIKELY BE:

A. Top banana.

B. Big cheese.

C. Something which couldn't be printed in books that may be read by children.

"QUITTING TIME" REFERS TO:

A. The culmination of your eight-hour workday.

B. When you finish the assigned task, even if it's after normal working hours.

C. The exact second your supervisor's eyes stop boring a hole in the back of your head, and your reflexes cause your feet to spring up onto your desk and your eyes to drift closed.

WHAT DO YOU SEE IN THIS PICTURE?

A. A pie chart.

B. The symbol for peace.

C. The hood ornament of the car the boss leaves early in.

Visual Acuity Test

Help the coworker find his glasses.

(HINT: They're on his head.)

YOU DON'T FEAR A CORPORATE TAKEOVER BID BECAUSE:
A. In today's economic climate, such a major financial undertaking seems unlikely.
B. Upper management at your company is too smart, savvy and streetwise.
C. People seldom try to board sinking ships.
76

TRUE or FALSE?

The copy machine is always broken.

FALSE! It's only broken when YOU need it.

WHEN FACED WITH A DIFFICULT BUSINESS DECISION, IT'S BEST TO:

A. Follow your acute instincts.

B. Consult with knowledgeable peers to get their opinions.

C. Go to the executive conference room and read the same tarot cards that management uses to guide its business decisions.

FILL IN THE BLANK!

All work and no play makes Jack a ______.

ANSWER: "boss's pet, who will snitch on you for those paper clips you took home and probably end up getting promoted."

Connect the dots!

Connect the dots to reveal the main reason you go to work in the morning.

BRAINTEASER

Which line for coffee is longer?

TRICK ANSWER! They're both the same length, until people on the left find out they're in the decaf line.

As people walk by your work area, they say:

A. "He's such a hard worker, he doesn't even look up."

B. "His concentration is so unwavering, he hasn't left his seat all day."

C. "Check his pulse!"

What's wrong with the following picture?

Answer: There's still enough money left over to buy food and clothing.

TRUE! But if you bring in a pillow, blanket and footie-pajamas, you're probably overdoing it.

Dividing up the check after a company lunch can be a trying experience, mainly because:

A. Nobody's any good at math.

B. Everyone's planning to pay with a credit card.

C. The marketing employees went to the bathroom and aren't coming back.

BRAIN TEASER!
Find the employee who left his lights on in the parking lot this morning.
★@~~,!!!
KLUNK!
OK... So it's not that tough...

CONNECT THE DOTS TO REVEAL WHAT YOUR COMPANY VALUES MOST.

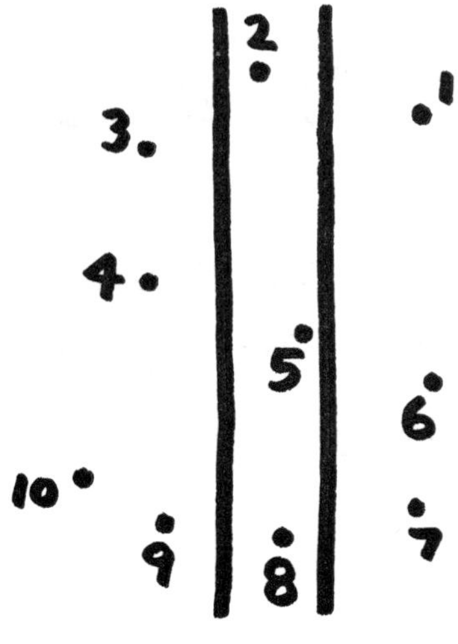

You go into the office restroom and discover there is no toilet paper. You immediately think:

A. Why isn't the custodial crew doing their job?

B. Maintenance would probably appreciate being notified.

C. Rats! Now I'll have to buy my own to use at home!

A. A valued, longtime employee of the company.

B. An employee nearing retirement.

C. An employee who called the home office when he was in his 20's, and has been on hold ever since.

FILL IN THE BLANK

A little hard work never ________ anyone.

Answer: "got done around here by"

Connect the Dots!

1. 2. .5

.4

3.

(Sure, it doesn't look like anything... but it kept you from having to work for a few minutes.)

Making long-distance personal calls at work is a crime punishable by:

A. Having to pay for them.

B. Having to pay for them and having to return stolen office supplies.

C. Having to pay for them and having to return stolen office supplies and having to move your car out of the spot reserved for visitors.

FILL IN THE BLANK
"If you don't get the ________ report on my desk by 5:00, heads are gonna roll!"
ANSWER: @mx?!!!

RIDDLE:

Why did the boss sit on the fence?

ANSWER: In order to have the best vantage point for videotaping employees leaving two minutes early.

WHICH IS THE MOST COMMON METHOD FOR RECYCLING PAPER AT YOUR WORKPLACE?

A. Paper is shredded and shipped to recycling plant.

B. Paper is collected in bins and shipped to recycling plants as is.

C. Making paper airplanes.

TRUE or FALSE
Management has your best interests at heart.
BOSS
FALSE! Management has no heart.